A Mexican Feast

The Foods and Recipes of Mexico

Ira Wood

Rosen
REAL
READERS

Rosen Classroom Books and Materials
New York

The recipes in this cookbook are intended for a child to make together with an adult.

Published in 2002 by The Rosen Publishing Group, Inc.
29 East 21st Street, New York, NY 10010

Book Design: Ron A. Churley

Photo Credits: Cover, p. 1 © Don Stevenson/Index Stock; p. 7 © SuperStock; pp. 8, 12, 14, 15, 19, 20 by Ron A. Churley; p. 10 © Cary Wolinsky/Stock, Boston/PictureQuest; p. 17 © Michelle Bridwell/PhotoEdit/PictureQuest; p. 22 © Danny Lehman/Corbis.

ISBN: 0-8239-8231-9
6-pack ISBN: 0-8239-8634-9

Manufactured in the United States of America

Contents

United
States

Mexico

Gulf of
Mexico

●
Mexico City

Pacific
Ocean

A Colorful Country

Mexico is the southernmost country in North America. It is the country to the south of the United States. To the east of Mexico is the Gulf of Mexico. To the west and south is the Pacific Ocean. The capital of Mexico is Mexico City. Over 8 million people live there!

Mexico is a large country with many different kinds of land. The north is rocky and has many mountains. The south has many rain forests. Mexico also has deserts, valleys, open plains, beautiful beaches, and **volcanoes**.

People have lived in the area that is now called Mexico for a long time. A group of North American Indians called the Maya (MY-uh) lived in southern Mexico between 1500 B.C. and 900 A.D.

About 100 million people live in Mexico.

We have found many works of art left from the ancient Maya, including pottery and paintings.

Another group of North American Indians called the Aztecs (AZ-teks) ruled southern Mexico between 1300 and 1500 A.D. The Aztecs built large cities all over the area that is known as southern Mexico today.

The Maya and the Aztecs both grew corn and chilies, or hot peppers. These two important Mexican foods are still grown and eaten today, thousands of years later.

Chilies have been an important food in Mexico for thousands of years. The Maya and Aztecs also grew tomatoes, corn, beans, and squash.

Trading Food

Explorers from Spain came to the land that is now called Mexico in the early 1500s. The Spanish and the Aztecs traded foods with each other. The Spanish brought the Aztecs cows, pigs, sheep, and goats. These were animals the Aztecs had never seen before.

The Spanish took Aztec foods—such as tomatoes, corn, beans, and sweet potatoes—back to Europe with them. These foods were then grown in Spain and Italy. They soon became a large part of European dishes.

Nachos, a tasty Mexican dish that is popular in the United States, are easy to make.

Nachos

You Will Need:

1 cup tomatoes, finely
chopped
1 green pepper,
seeded and diced
2 jalapeño peppers,
diced
1/2 cup chopped
scallions
2 cups grated
Monterey Jack
cheese
1 12-ounce bag tortilla
chips
black olives, sliced
guacamole
salsa
sour cream

How to Do It:

Heat oven to 350°F. In
a bowl, mix tomatoes,
peppers, and scallions.
Cover a baking sheet
with foil. Place layer of
chips on the baking
sheet. Sprinkle cheese
evenly over chips. Bake
for 10 minutes, or until
cheese has melted.
Spread tomato mixture
and black olives over
cheese and chips. Serve
on a large tray with
guacamole, salsa, and
sour cream for dipping.
Serves 4 to 6.

Popular Mexican Foods

One of the most popular Mexican foods is a flat bread called a tortilla (tor-TEE-yah). Tortillas can be made with corn or wheat flour. Many Mexican families eat them with every meal.

Corn tortillas are made by grinding corn and mixing it with water until it forms a dough. This dough is rolled into flat, thin bread. The bread is then fried in a pan over a fire. After tortillas are cooked, they are ready to be eaten.

Tortillas can be eaten alone or with a mixture of foods wrapped inside them, including tomatoes, beans, meat, and cheese. This tasty bread is also used to make tacos and **burritos**.

The people of Mexico have grown corn for thousands of years. It has become one of their

Mexican people have been making tortillas for thousands of years. Even the Maya ate tortillas with most of their meals.

most important foods. Many Mexican dishes have corn in them. Corn is sometimes dried and crushed to make cornmeal, which can then be used in many recipes. There is even a thick drink made from cornmeal, called *atole* (ah-TOH-lay).

Beans are another popular Mexican food. They are often boiled, mashed, and then fried to make tasty dishes. Rice is also boiled and fried. Sweet potatoes, tomatoes, and **avocados** are also common foods in Mexico today.

Hot chilies make many Mexican dishes, like tacos and burritos, very spicy.

Mexican people often grow and dry their own **herbs** and chilies to use while cooking. These add a spicy flavor to Mexican dishes.

Soft Tacos

You Will Need:

1 lb. ground beef
1/4 cup water
1 small onion, diced
1/2 tsp. salt
1/2 tsp. black pepper
1/2 tsp. garlic powder
1/2 tsp. ground cumin
10 six-inch tortillas
3 large tomatoes,
    diced
1 head of lettuce,
    shredded
1/2 cup chopped
    black olives
2 cups cheddar
    cheese, grated
guacamole
salsa
sour cream

How to Do It:

Brown beef in a pan over medium heat. When the beef is no longer pink, drain fat and add water, onion, and spices. Mix well while cooking over medium heat. Stir occasionally. Place tomatoes, lettuce, olives, cheese, guacamole, salsa, and sour cream in separate dishes. When the water is gone from the beef, remove the pan from the heat. Spoon 1–2 tablespoons of beef into the center of each tortilla. Add toppings and wrap. Serves 8 to 10.

Mexican foods are often as colorful as they are good to eat. Sauces add color and flavor to many **traditional** Mexican dishes. One favorite Mexican sauce is **guacamole** (gwah-kuh-

Guacamole is a bright green sauce.

MOH-lee), which is made from mashed avocados. Salsa is another popular Mexican sauce. Salsa is a spicy sauce made with tomatoes, onion, and chilies. Guacamole and salsa are both used as a dip for nachos or as a topping for tacos and other dishes.

Salsa can be made very spicy by adding chilies.

Salsa

You Will Need:

2 tbsps. olive oil
1/2 small onion, finely
   chopped
1/3 cup fresh cilantro,
   chopped, or 1
   tbsp. dried cilantro
2 medium tomatoes,
   finely chopped
1/2 tsp. oregano
2 garlic cloves, minced
2 tsps. red wine vinegar
1/2 tsp. salt
1/2 green pepper, diced
1 12-ounce bag tortilla
   chips

How to Do It:

In a medium-sized
frying pan, heat olive oil
over medium-high heat.
Add onion and garlic.
Cook until they are clear,
about 2 to 3 minutes.
Remove from heat. Add
the rest of the ingredients
and mix well. You can
mash up the tomatoes
if you like. Chill for 3
hours. Serve with
tortilla chips. Serves
4 to 6.

Mexican Mealtime

In Mexico, mealtime is more than just a time to eat food. It is a time for families to come together and enjoy each other's company. Some Mexican families eat five meals a day. This allows them to spend a lot of time together. In large cities, most people eat only three meals a day.

For traditional Mexican families, the first meal is an early breakfast, followed by a light mid-morning meal around eleven o'clock in the morning. The main meal of the day is eaten around two in the afternoon. At seven o'clock in the evening, Mexican families have a light snack. Later, they have a light dinner before they go to bed. All these meals give Mexican families a lot of time to be together.

In Mexico, meals are an important time of the day. Families take the time to share a meal together.

In Mexico, the main meal of the day is the *comida* (koh-MEE-dah). This meal starts around two in the afternoon and lasts for two or three hours. During *comida,* shops and stores close so people can enjoy this meal at home with their families.

Comida often starts with soup. Many Mexican people eat *sopa de arroz,* or rice soup. This meal also includes a side dish of rice and beans, and a main dish, such as *pollo en salsa verde,* or chicken in green sauce. Vegetables are also served with this meal. To finish *comida,* Mexican families have a dessert, such as flan or hot chocolate.

Sopa de arroz is easy to make, but always ask a grown-up to help you when you use a stove or an oven.

Sopa de Arroz

You Will Need:

2 tbsps. vegetable oil
2/3 cup cooked rice
1 clove garlic, minced
1 medium onion,
   chopped
1 green chili pepper,
   chopped
3 tomatoes, chopped
4 cups beef or chicken
   stock
1 1/2 tsps. salt

How to Do It:

Heat oil in a deep saucepan over medium heat. Add rice, garlic, onion, and chili pepper. Fry until brown, stirring often. Add tomatoes, stock, and salt. Simmer for 20 minutes. Serve hot. Serves 4.

Mexican Treats

In Mexico, *comida* is not over until after dessert. One of the most popular desserts is flan, a type of **custard** covered with a **caramel** shell. This is a special treat for Mexican children. Hot chocolate is another popular dessert. Sweet treats are also served during Mexican **celebrations**, such as *Dia de los Muertos,* or Day of

When making flan, the hot caramel will burn you if it gets on your skin. Let a grown-up do this part.

the Dead. On November 1, Mexican families remember friends and family members who have died. Special treats in the shape of colorful skulls are made for this celebration.

Flan

You Will Need:

3/4 cup sugar
4 eggs
1 tsp. vanilla extract
1 can sweetened
    condensed milk
1 can evaporated milk

How to Do It:

Heat the sugar in a small pot over medium heat. Stir occasionally for 12 to 15 minutes. When the sugar turns to a golden liquid, reduce heat to low and stir frequently. When the sugar turns dark brown, remove from heat and quickly pour into a 9-inch cake pan. Turn the pan to coat the sides with caramel, then set aside to cool. Mix the eggs, vanilla extract, condensed milk, and evaporated milk in a bowl. Pour the mixture over the caramel. Place cake pan in a large pan of water and bake for one hour at 350°F. Add boiling water to the pan if the water level gets low. Cool flan, then put in refrigerator. Unmold flan onto a plate before serving, caramel side up. Serves about 10.

Around the World with Mexican Food

Tortilla chips, refried beans, salsa, nachos, and tacos are popular in many different countries. Tex-Mex and Southwestern cooking are styles of Mexican cooking mixed with American styles. Chili con carne, a stew made with beans, meat, and chilies, is made with Mexican flavors.

Mexican foods are served in restaurants and stores all around the world.

You can use the recipes in this book to make a Mexican meal for your friends and family to enjoy. As they say in Mexico, *buen provecho*! (Enjoy!)

Glossary

avocado	A green fruit that is about the size of a pear and has thick skin.
burrito	A Mexican dish with meat, beans, cheese, and vegetables wrapped in a large tortilla.
caramel	A sticky brown candy made by heating sugar until it melts.
celebration	A special event honoring something important.
custard	A firm pudding made with milk and eggs.
explorer	A person who travels to new lands to find new things.
guacamole	A thick sauce made from mashed avocados.
herb	A plant used for seasoning foods.
traditional	The way a group of people has done something for a long time.
volcano	An opening in the Earth's crust through which melted rock is sometimes forced.

Index